If you were a
Capital Letter

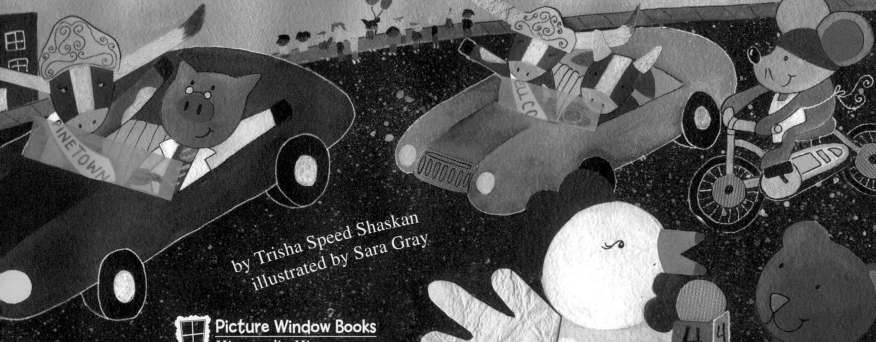

by Trisha Speed Shaskan
illustrated by Sara Gray

Picture Window Books
Minneapolis, Minnesota

capital letter an uppercase letter used at the beginning of sentences and proper nouns

Editor: Jill Kalz
Designer: Abbey Fitzgerald
Page Production: Melissa Kes
Art Director: Nathan Gassman
Editorial Director: Nick Healy
Creative Director: Joe Ewest
The illustrations in this book were created with acrylics.

Picture Window Books
151 Good Counsel Drive
P.O. Box 669
Mankato, MN 56002-0669
877-845-8392
www.picturewindowbooks.com

Printed in the United States of America.

 All books published by Picture Window Books
are manufactured with paper containing at least
10 percent post-consumer waste.

Library of Congress Cataloging-in-Publication Data
Shaskan, Trisha Speed, 1973–
If you were a capital letter / by Trisha Speed Shaskan ;
illustrated by Sara Gray.
p. cm. — (Word fun)
Includes index.
ISBN 978-1-4048-5515-1 (library binding)
ISBN 978-1-4048-5694-3 (paperback)
1. English language—Capitalization—Juvenile literature.
2. Reporting—Juvenile literature. I. Gray, Sara, ill.
II. Title.
PE1450.S423 2009
428.1—dc22   2009002705

Special thanks to our advisers for their expertise:

Rosemary G. Palmer, Ph.D., Literacy Consultant

Terry Flaherty, Ph.D., Professor of English
Minnesota State University, Mankato

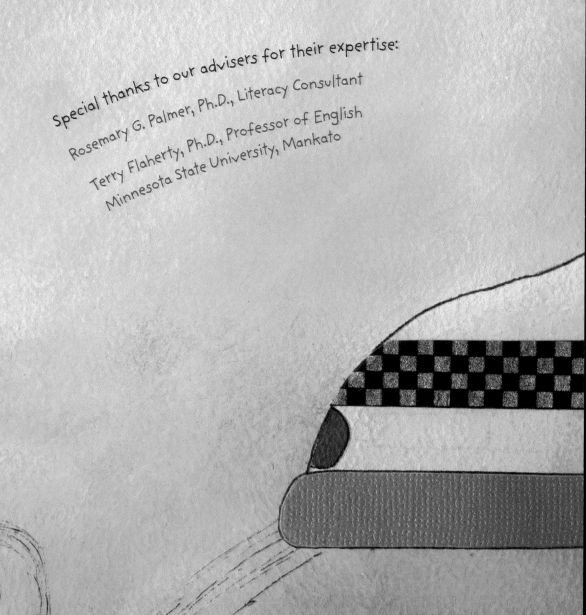

If you were a capital letter ...

TAXI

New York City
Taxi Company

3

... you would stand out.

Staten Island Ferry

Penny Pecksworth and her family enjoy the last day of their New York City vacation. They ride the Staten Island Ferry. They see the Statue of Liberty.

If you were a capital letter, you would be the first letter of a person's first, middle, and last names.

Monday morning, back in Texas, Penny Ann Pecksworth and Frank Boris Furter are late for work.

Dr. Frank Furter

But Marty Lewis Mouse is right on time.

6

If you were a capital letter, you would be the first letter in a sentence.

The interview is about to start. Crew members fix Penny's feathers and make-up.

8

They fix Frank's tie.

Dr. Frank Furter

If you were a capital letter, you would be the first letter of a direct quote. A direct quote is the exact words someone says.

Penny Pecksworth asks her guest, "What advice can you give our viewers?"

"Eating breakfast is *egg-stra* important!" he says.

If you were a capital letter, you would be the first letter of a person's title, such as Dr. (Doctor), Mr. (Mister), or Mrs. (Missus).

"You are such a ham, **D**r. Furter!" Penny says.

If you were a capital letter, you would be the first letter of a salutation, or greeting. You would also be the first letter of a closing.

Dear Dr. Frank Furter,

I caught the tail-end of your interview on TV. Eggs are good for breakfast, but so is cheese! I like cheddar best.

Yours truly,
Marty L. Mouse

If you were a capital letter, you would be the first letter of a proper noun. A proper noun is the name of a specific person, place, or thing.

Austin, Texas, has a Fourth of July parade each year. It follows Sixth Street.

The princess from Pine Town rides in a red car.
The princess from Bell County rides in a blue car.

If you were a capital letter, you would be the first letter of each day of the week and each month of the year.

Sunday	Monday	Tuesday	Wednesday	Thursday	Friday	Saturday
				1	2	3
4	5	6	7	8	9	10
11	12	13	14	15	16	17
18	19	20	21	22	23	24
25	26	27	28	29	30	31

Penny's birthday falls on a **Monday** this year. Her birthday is **January** 26.

If you were a capital letter, you would be the first letter of a holiday.

Marty's favorite holiday is Halloween.

18

Dr. Frank Furter's favorite holiday is Thanksgiving.

Penny's favorite holiday is **May Day**.

19

If you were a capital letter, you would be the first letter of the major words in a movie title, song title, or book title.

Dr. Frank Furter always wanted to be an actor. Last year, he starred in the musical "Pig in a Blanket."

THEATER

Pig in a Blanket

Starring Dr. Frank Furter

Box Office

He sang the song
"Making My Pig Debut."

This year, he wrote a book called *From Runt to Rising Star.*

From Runt to Rising Star

From Runt to

If you were a capital letter ...

... you would make it big!

A CAPITAL IDEA

What you need:

- a magazine or newspaper article
- a yellow marker or highlighter

What you do:

Read the article. Next, use the marker to highlight each capital letter you find. Figure out why the letters you've highlighted are capitalized. Is the letter at the beginning of a sentence or proper noun? Does the letter begin a direct quote? If you can't figure it out, look back through this book, and see if you can find the answer.

Glossary

capital letter—an uppercase letter used at the beginning of sentences and proper nouns

direct quote—the exact words someone says

noun—a word that names a person, place, or thing

proper noun—a word that names a specific person, place, or thing

salutation—a greeting

title—a word or group of words used to show a person's position or job; also, the name of a book, story, song, or other work of art

To Learn More

More Books to Read

Scheunemann, Pam. *Places*. Edina, Minn.: Abdo, 2001.

Wood, Audrey. *Alphabet Mystery*. New York: Blue Sky Press, 2003.

Wood, Audrey. *Alphabet Rescue*. New York: Scholastic, 2006.

Internet Sites

FactHound offers a safe, fun way to find Internet sites related to this book. All of the sites on FactHound have been researched by our staff.

Here's all you do:

Visit **www.facthound.com**

FactHound will fetch the best sites for you!

Index

closings, 13

days of the week, 16

direct quotes, 10, 23

greetings, 13

holidays, 18, 19

months, 16

names, 6, 14

proper nouns, 14, 23

sentences, 8, 23

titles, 11, 20

Look for all of the books in the Word Fun series:

If You Were a Capital Letter
If You Were a Comma
If You Were a Compound Word
If You Were a Conjunction
If You Were a Contraction
If You Were a Homonym or a Homophone
If You Were a Noun
If You Were a Palindrome
If You Were a Period
If You Were a Plural Word
If You Were a Prefix
If You Were a Preposition
If You Were a Pronoun
If You Were a Question Mark
If You Were a Suffix
If You Were a Synonym
If You Were a Verb
If You Were Alliteration
If You Were an Adjective
If You Were an Adverb
If You Were an Antonym
If You Were an Apostrophe
If You Were an Exclamation Point
If You Were an Interjection
If You Were Onomatopoeia
If You Were Quotation Marks